Mothers of Exceptional Children

The Journey, The Joy and The Plight of Real Advocacy

Mothers of Exceptional Children
The Journey, The Joy and The Plight of Real Advocacy

Written By:
Abena Asantewa, Angela Williams, Cheryl Barnes,
Nycole Buckner, Khadija Ali, and Sharalene Wheeler

© 2022 Mothers of Exceptional Children- The Journey, The Joy and The Plight of Real Advocacy
Cover design and illustration: Yolanda A. Barnes (Yogii)
Editor, proof-reading: Alkebulan Andrea Foster
Authors: Abena Asantewa, Angela Williams, Cheryl Barnes, Nycole Buckner, Khadija Ali, Sharalene Wheeler
Publisher: MOEC Publishing
ISBN Paperback: 978-0-578-56889-8

Table of Contents

Exceptional One 1
Introduction by Dr. Abena Asantewaa 2
   Biography 8
   Acknowledgements 9
Welcome To Jamir Speaks by Nycole Buckner 10
   Biography 27
   Acknowledgements 28
The Extraordinary Mr. Miles by Cheryl Barnes 30
   Biography 42
   Acknowledgements 43
Unexpected Blessing by Angela Williams 46
   Biography 58
   Acknowledgements 60
Goose Lucy-The Greatest Teacher by Khadija Ali 62
   Biography 69
   Acknowledgements 70
The UP Side of Downs by Sharalene Wheeler 74
   Biography 88
   Acknowledgements 90
Resources 92
To The Reader 96

Exceptional One

Original Author: Unknown
Readapted by: Sharalene Wheeler-Reaves
for Kameron Mattox

Exceptional One

The child, yet unborn, spoke with Creator and said, 'Mother, how will I survive in the world? I will not be like other Children, my walk may be slower, my speech will be hard to understand, I will look, think and process differently. What is to become of me?

The Creator replied, 'OH, my Precious Precious One, have no fear, I have given you exceptional super powers? You will be able to teach the world how to love unconditionally. You will have the power to bring a smile to every face and soften every heart that you encounter. Just by your presence you will show the world the beauty in every person I have created differently. I will give you exceptional parents that will guide, protect and marvel in your accomplishments, they will learn to love you because you are special, not in spite of it.

Though others on the outside may see your path throughout life as difficult, your reward will be greater. You have been blessed with a special ability to love, and those whose lives you touch will be blessed because you are special"

Special Education 101

Abena Asantewaa, Ph.D.

If you have a child with a physical, emotional or intellectual disability, you will need to be your child's strongest advocate. Among other challenges, you will probably need to navigate the special education system.

Special education is complicated, and full of unfamiliar language and requirements. You will probably sit through meetings where everyone in the room understands the system and terminology, except you. A PTE? PWN? C setting? Who's on the team – just the school staff, or are you on the team, too? You may feel like you and your child are being railroaded, or like your concerns are not being addressed. Many times, you're right.

IDEA

IDEA (the Individuals with Disabilities Education Act) is a set of federal regulations that govern special education. The aim of IDEA is to provide for a Free and Appropriate Public Education (FAPE) for every student. While individual states may vary a little in how they interpret and implement IDEA, they have to adhere to it or risk losing huge amounts of federal funding. The more you understand the areas of IDEA that apply to your child, the stronger you will be. The worst mistake you can make is to sit passively and assume that the educators know what your child needs, and trust them to act in your child's best interest.

PRE-REFERRAL

Special education shouldn't be Plan A for every child who needs extra help. Depending on your child's needs, the school may be able to make adjustments in the regular classroom, using the general education curriculum, and still accommodate him or her. The goal should be to have each student in the Least Restrictive Environment (LRE – another term from IDEA). There are countless extras that children in a general education class enjoy, from socializing with a variety of peers to science experiments and field trips, that children in self-contained, special education classes usually miss out on. Schools have systems in place to identify children with special needs, and provide extra assistance in the general education classroom.

The Student Assistance Team (or some similar name) meets at least once a month to discuss students whom teachers have identified as struggling, either academically or socially. They agree on strategies to support them in their areas of need, and report back in 8-12 weeks to see if the student is showing improvement. If the child is making significant progress toward grade-level performance, the strategies will continue, and no further steps will be taken. In its formalized version, this approach is known as Response to Intervention, or RtI. If the child is responding well to intervention at the general education level, they will probably not be referred for special education. If they are not making progress within 3 - 6 months, the process should go to the next level.

If you already have a diagnosis and know that you want your child to receive services, you can bypass the pre-referral stage. The quickest approach is to write a letter requesting an evaluation. Address the letter to the principal and keep a copy for yourself. Make sure to date it. Don't be surprised if you get a bit of a run-around, but by law they have to abide by your request for testing. At the very least, you should be advised that the school has considered it, and their reasons for accepting or rejecting your request. If they have chosen not to evaluate your child, ask for their reasons in writing.

REFERRAL
Students who continue to struggle, and are not showing improvement, may be referred for evaluation. This entire process, and everything that follows, is covered by IDEA. The school psychologist, and other staff (different states and school districts have different names for them) have steps they have to take, forms they have to complete, and timelines they have to adhere to.

The first step should be to meet with you, discuss the concerns they have, and ask for your permission to evaluate your child. The PTE (Permission to Evaluate) form should identify what areas they wish to evaluate (intellectual ability, academic achievement, social-emotional functioning, autism, health-related concerns) and offer a date by which this evaluation will be completed. At this time, you should also be offered a brochure called Procedural Safeguards, which sets out your child's rights, your rights as a parent, and some outside sources of information and advocacy. You are well within your rights to ask for a bit of time so that you can fully understand what you are signing.

As soon as you receive the Permission to Evaluate form, you should buy an accordion folder (office supply stores have them) so that you can keep EVERY SINGLE document that you receive from the school concerning your child and the special education process. **Everything you sign is a legal document.**

EVALUATION AND ELIGIBILITY

Once you have given your permission, the school psychologist will evaluate your child, and write a multidisciplinary report. It's called multidisciplinary because it should reflect input from several sources. You will be asked to complete a developmental history that includes information regarding your pregnancy, ages when your child reached developmental milestones (sitting, walking, toilet training) as well as medical history and family composition. His or her teacher(s) will be asked about academic strengths and weaknesses, and behavior concerns. Other professionals may be asked to assess his or her speech or motor skills.

When the report is complete, you and the teachers and related professionals will meet to go over the results. At this meeting, your child's eligibility for special education services will be determined. Federal law lays out the eligibility criteria for each of the areas in which a child can qualify for services. These criteria may differ from what your doctor used to make a diagnosis. Even with a clear diagnosis, your child may not meet state criteria, because there is a difference between a medical diagnosis and an educational disability.

(An educational disability is one that interferes with the child's ability to benefit from the regular curriculum in the general education classroom.) The team has to agree that the child qualifies for services in order to move forward, and then you are asked to sign off. To clarify, you are a member of the team. If you are not in agreement, you don't have to sign. But at that point, you probably want some outside help.

The results of the evaluation are valid for three years. By the anniversary date, the law requires that your child should be re-evaluated to determine if he or she continues to qualify for services.

THE IEP
Once the team agrees that your child qualifies for services, an educational plan is developed. Usually this meeting immediately follows the eligibility determination, but they are actually two separate steps and can be done at different times. The IEP (Individual Educational Plan) lays out the needs the school proposes to address in the next year.

Don't take the IEP lightly, because it is a legally binding contract stating what the school district will do for your child. My suggestion is that you study it and understand it before you sign it. If something is mentioned, it has to be done. If something is not mentioned, they don't have to do it. For example, if your child needs a one-on-one paraprofessional to accompany him or her all day, make sure it's stated in the IEP – don't assume that anything will be done if it isn't in writing.

The IEP is updated once a year, and your child's progress in meeting the goals from the previous year are reviewed. If you transfer your child to another school district, you should give the new school a copy of the most recent IEP, so they know what your child needs. Sometimes it takes months for the paperwork to get from one district to another. If you wait for the school to do it, and your child may not get the services they need in the meanwhile. See why you needed that accordion folder?

Biography

"It is easier to build strong children than to repair broken men."
Frederick Douglass

Dr. Abena Asantewaa is a clinical and school psychologist, with a postgraduate degree in each area from Adelphi University and 40 years of experience. She is the "Black Boy Advocate", with a website of that name.

"Dr. A" has taught a variety of psychology courses, primarily in Child Development, at schools ranging from the University of Notre Dame and the City University of New York, to the University of Ghana and Ashesi University in Ghana.

She directed the largest battered women's shelter in New York City.

Dr. A has served as a school psychologist in a variety of school districts, throughout the U.S. and in Ghana, West Africa. Recently retired, she now pursues her passions of advocating for Black boys, and addressing issues of race and gender in the classroom. She is currently writing a book with the working title, In Defense of Black Boys. It addresses the "School to Prison Pipeline", disproportionately high rates of severe discipline, and inclusion in special education, offering insights from both academic research and the author's personal experience as a school psychologist and the
 Black mother of Black sons.

Her previous book, Letter to My Teacher: Insights into Special Needs Students, is available in digital format on Amazon. It is an introduction to the major categories of special needs students that general education teachers may encounter, advising them how to work with those students in a compassionate and productive manner. It includes an extensive bibliography for further reference, and is suitable for parents as well as teachers.

Acknowledgments

I am thankful for all the people and all the experiences I've encountered. Everything in my life has made me who I am.

As I settle into my 70's, and my role as Elder,
my perspective is changing.
Here is what I'm learning:

There is something to be thankful for in every situation. The happy ones give me pleasure; the difficult ones offer lessons
 (if I choose to learn them).

Painful experiences provide the fuel for growth. In 70+ years, I haven't found a way to grow without pain (trust me, I've tried.)

When I thank God for whatever is happening,
 in time it yields a blessing.

Thank you, Khadija Wilson, for inviting me into this community. When my life experience can help someone else navigate theirs, it becomes gratitude-worthy. So as my African friends put it,
I thank God for my life.

Introduction

My name is Paul Jamir Hutchins, better known as "PJ" or "Jamir," and I have autism. I am considered non-verbal, yet I can communicate my needs, and I do speak when I find it necessary. Some professionals believe people with autism can use the condition or diagnosis to their advantage, especially when there is a need to tune out the world. I consider it a sense of freedom and make a conscious effort to enjoy EVERY moment of my life.

But this story is about my mom and the challenges that she has faced parenting an African American son with autism. I am sure she could write volumes but have chosen the more notable experiences that she deemed most important in my development. Many of these occurrences have radically shaped or even redefined the approach and protocols put in place to support me. As a 27-year-old African American young man with epilepsy, on the autism spectrum, this is my mother's story. I invite you to spend a moment with us on our journey.

Birth: May Your Boy Bring You, Joy

My name is Nycole, and in 1994, Paul and I became pregnant with our first child. The baby would be due in December, around Christmas and my birthday. Both families were ecstatic!! So much to look forward to around the holiday season. I started receiving prenatal care in my first trimester and read everything I could about pregnancy and birth, hoping to have an uneventful pregnancy and a healthy baby. It wasn't difficult to get the professional support I needed because my mother was a certified nurse-midwife and unit director of labor and delivery at Rush Presbyterian St. Luke Medical Center. So, I was placed in the hands of knowledgeable and caring professionals and had a loving and caring family support system...what could go wrong?

On December 22nd, I was admitted to the hospital for labor induction. Yes, that is close to Christmas and my birthday. It is an understatement to say that my family was excited: Twelve people were present for my birth. Further, the timing was just right because Paul, an offensive lineman for the Green Bay Packers, was able to catch a flight from Tampa to be there in time for his birth. I experienced what I perceive to be a beautiful and prolonged labor and, on December 23rd, 1994, gave birth to my first child.... It's a boy!!! We would later learn that there is a higher incidence of males diagnosed with Autism Spectrum Disorder.

We named our son Paul Jamir as his birth represented the beginning of a fourth-generational legacy. Not only were our family members excited to welcome him into this world, but they were also ready to welcome him into his birthright in his family lineage. Ultimately, Jamir would become the first of many titles in our family, reigning as the first great-grandson, grandson, great-nephew, and nephew. Ultimately, for Paul and me, he would be our first and only child.

Although I don't know Jim Carey, I am sending him a massive shout-out. Much to my surprise, watching Jim Carey's portrayal of his comedic role in the film Ace Ventura Pet Detective in the birthing center would not only begin my labor process but would greatly provide ease to support and distract the pains that come with labor and delivery. Humor was a great source of relief and a potential remedy during labor. Maintaining such laughter helped distract me from the pains I would endure over the next several hours. Through each contraction, Paul, my brother Erik, and I continued to chime, "I just can't do it, Captain, I don't have the power!" I genuinely give Jim Carey the credit for helping make the journey of delivering my son a little less painful. Thank you, Mr. Carey, for bringing more joy and relaxation to my birthing process.

Diagnosis

From birth, PJ was a happy baby and warmed the hearts of all who loved him. He met his milestones with flying colors: cooing, smiling (he made good eye contact), laughing, and yes, talking: he recited the alphabet in its entirety, sang full lyrics to songs and nursery rhymes, and indicate his wants and needs in 3-4 word sentences. One of his favorite things to say was "Leave me la-lone". I remember saying, "Wow, he's pretty precocious, perhaps even gifted. However, as I reflect, PJ did exhibit a few behaviors that concerned me.

He appeared to focus intensely on objects for an extended period. For example, while sitting in his infant carrier at seven weeks old, he was attentive to the NCAA basketball game on television. I recall asking his father a few times, "Is he watching this game so intently at 7 weeks old? Is he tracking the basketball at such a young age?" I didn't think this was possible, but I stood and watched his eyes as he tracked and continued to follow the basketball. Ironically, he later became very interested in basketball and, occasionally, can shoot baskets with his eyes closed. Also, at one point, I recall thinking my son was hard of hearing, as sometimes, he did not appear to respond when I would call him by his name. On many occasions, I would test to see if he could hear by standing behind him and clapping to see if I would receive a response. Most times, he would respond, but there were those times he did not. This greatly concerned me, but I was reassured by his pediatrician and family that he was fine.

PJ was 18 months old when he began demonstrating more "odd" behaviors. One day, while holding his sippy cup near the refrigerator, his phrase "juice please" became "Less lees". From that day, I would see significant regression. There was a decline in his level of communication. He didn't appear to "need" either of his parents in the manner he once displayed. Initially, Jamir would reach out to us to help or tend to his wants or needs. Now he was aloof and became someone independent at a time when pre-toddlers needed support from their parents. Essentially, he began to use language less and point or motion toward desired objects.

During this same timeframe, his early childhood teacher, who had recently advanced him into the 2-year-old class at 18 months, had made an interesting note. She indicated that Jamir was no longer socially engaging with his peers: She said there were incidents where Jamir would not share or exchange toys with the other children. In hindsight, not socializing and engaging with peers was a significant trait or characteristic for youth on the autism spectrum. As I continued to read the teacher's note, my heart sank! As a mother, it was one thing for me to notice these irregular behaviors that Jamir had displayed with me at home. Still, when his teacher observed similar behaviors in her classroom, it confirmed that this wasn't in my head and that my son was regressing. The teacher's note validated all my suspicions regarding my son, and I knew he would require a thorough evaluation. This would be the first time someone outside of myself would indicate notable concerns regarding Jamir.

PJ also began throwing horrible temper tantrums: He would fall out on the floor and screech like a wounded animal. He would display this behavior at home as well as in public. One can only imagine how heartbroken and frightened I was. What was happening to my baby? People didn't know much about autism then and were very insensitive. I would overhear people mutter "if that were my child I would..." And you can imagine all the hurtful things that were said. Commonly people would refer to PJ as a spoiled brat who needed his butt beat!!! One of my worse experiences was during Christmas when I went to the mall to have his picture taken with Santa Claus. PJ threw one of his temper tantrums, knocking over candy cane and lollipop props as other children and their families looked on in horror. Then PJ took off running through the mall with the speed of Usain Bolt. Of course, I had to endure the comments from the onlookers about "what that boy needed". What that boy, my son, needed was a diagnosis! What that boy, my son, needed was a mother who was going to support and advocate for him. What the public needed was more compassion and not be judgmental with children who may have special needs. I would later learn that PJ was having "meltdowns," which are common in children with autism. I would later learn techniques to calm and comfort him. But at this point, we didn't have a diagnosis.

While taking an undergraduate course in developmental psychology at the University of Illinois, Chicago, I learned about autism. In a tiny subsection of my developmental psychology text, there was a brief description pertaining to autism disorders. As I intensely perused this section, I felt like what I read most emphatically described the behaviors and concerns I witnessed with my son. During class, I read and reread this section several times before jumping out of my seat and heading toward my professor near the front of the lecture hall. I desperately wanted to learn more as it pertained to autism. Reading this section on this day was a defining moment for my son and me, as I now had a name for this phenomenon. A clinical term for what described in detail my son's behaviors and responsive interactions.

PJ's dad and I had our son evaluated by several pediatricians, yet none would say definitively that PJ had autism. Despite their full support in providing a medical referral to a top pediatric neurology specialist, they concluded that my son's behavior was self-stimulating and something he might outgrow. One physician indicated that "my son's uncontrollable rocking was similar to a child sucking his thumb." Although I believed and respected their roles as my son's pediatric team, I disagreed with their medical conclusions and felt my questions were left unanswered. I would leave their offices with no real answers or tangible solutions. However, this time, I left with the referral they provided for the pediatric neurologist. I immediately scheduled my son's appointment, which would take place TEN MONTHS later.

While I anticipated meeting with this top pediatric neurologist, I relentlessly sought the support of other professionals, including developmental specialists, speech therapists, educators, peers, professors, and colleagues. In hindsight, I had officially created a comprehensive team that would address and offer the support structure I desperately needed to have in place for Jamir.

I continued to document names of specialists to follow up with and call various pediatric organizations; I strategically set up appointments to take my son. I was heartbroken and frightened, yet I knew that I had to keep investigating. My beautiful, precious baby!!! Could someone please HELP OUR SON! I created a timeline listing all the behaviors I saw my son display, indicating the patterns, frequency, and places the behaviors occurred. I also took videos of his behaviors to share with the professional community. I kept these detailed accounts in a binder so that as we met and spoke with specialists, I would have accurate documentation to share. By now, our family and I were sure PJ had autism. All we wanted was a professional diagnosis.

A Mother's Instinct: I just knew he needed help
As I continued to observe and compiled notes on my son, I saw even more distinctive patterns that glaringly suggested that my son would

require additional support. I knew that my son required more, WAY MORE and that early intervention would be critical in his development.

Honestly, there were days I felt hopeless. It felt like my Jamir was regressing before my eyes, and I was not provided with any answers or plausible solutions. This made my experience even more painful. I felt like I was losing my son to something I couldn't fully grasp or even understand. I was perplexed because I could not comprehend what was happening to him, and right before my very eyes.

As a family, we felt like we were in this silo trying to figure out how to best support our son. Being in this silo meant we were left to deal with this alone; at times, it was lonely. I couldn't just call on my pediatrician or a family friend and ask for advice on how to deal with things as they would occur with Jamir. He was a unique being. Autism was not yet described as the entity it is today, where constant awareness, research, and media attention were brought forth.

As a mother, my job is to protect my son at all costs, yet I felt helpless because there were no answers. As a student studying psychology and working with youth and small children for some time, I knew something was uniquely compelling about my son's behaviors. In my heart, I felt that the behaviors I was seeing indicated autism. I did what was within my power to do. I prayed, continued to take copious notes on and about Jamir, read through the literature, and sought the professionals who I thought were most knowledgeable on autism. I spoke to anyone who could or would address my inquiries to help me help my son.

The appointment that we had anticipated for ten months had now finally arrived. We were excited because we would proceed with what we deemed the most crucial medical evaluation to best serve our son. After seeing the pediatric neurologist and completing tests, doing written consultations, and meeting with the team, we would finally get the support we had been trying so hard to attain. After a day of observation, definitive tests, and copious clinical notes, the top pediatric neurologist and his team determine their findings. The specialist contacted Paul via telephone and shared his diagnosis. He indicated that his findings were inconclusive and that our son was too sociable to have autism. After waiting for the specialist opinion, our suspicions were not confirmed. I felt defeated AGAIN! After waiting ten months for a specialist to render a diagnosis...it was inconclusive!

The physician's claim was supposedly based on the series of tests and how friendly Jamir appeared. He was too sociable, smiling, and laughing, and his ability to provide direct eye contact meant that our son did not have autism. This conversation, which I was not privy to, took place over the phone with his father, not me. I continued to contact this specialist as I had additional follow-up questions.

Additionally, had I ever had an opportunity to speak with him directly, I would have liked to discuss his findings and request a referral for a second opinion. To this very day, this doctor has NEVER returned my phone calls. I recall feeling so defeated! Despite our best efforts to find out, we still had no diagnosis.

REAL Advocacy
During the early 1990s, many resources serving individuals with autism were unavailable, especially for people of color. No one was discussing autism in the manner we see today. I do not recall many practitioners specializing in autism or autism spectrum disorders. For those medical professionals who specialized in autism, securing an appointment with them often meant being scheduled a year to a year-and-a-half out. That was even more discouraging for me, as many youths of color go undiagnosed and do not receive the necessary early interventions. Some specialists would only agree to meet or assess clients within the three-year and 11-months age parameters for reasons still unknown to me today. Jamir was already two years and some months old when I began locating specialists and scheduling such appointments.

When one discusses advocacy, particularly for children of color, this sends me to another level that is often not amply discussed. Individuals and families of color are often forced to navigate different treatment levels while seeking optimal services (medical, educational, social, etc.) for their loved ones. Cultural humility has yet to be our experience in dealing with various types of professionals from multiple organizations while seeking support for our son. And thankfully, we had the means both educationally and financially. I can only imagine the trauma experienced by families with limited resources. The conversation and discourse for families of color acquiring and receiving resources deserve an entire book, not a chapter. However, I will continue to mandate that YOU advocate for your child(ren) no matter what! You must continue fighting across such systems until you and your loved ones get the necessary support.

When we didn't receive an official diagnosis of autism from the pediatric neurologist, I proceeded with the next available course of action. I visited the Midlothian School District (a school district outside of our residence) to have PJ evaluated. In this process, I knew a team of school professionals would conduct a comprehensive educational evaluation, determining my son's needs based on his strengths and challenges. Compared to the recent medical review, I believe the educational evaluation would respect my role as a viable entity in my son's world. My observations and questions were critical to this educational evaluative process; I felt valued and heard. I finally had the team.

This team was dynamic and comprehensive in their approach and extraordinarily patient and kind as they walked Paul and me step-by-step through this process. This group of clinicians, including a school psychologist, special education case manager, and school administrator from the district, convened for pre-, co-, and post-evaluation. They each took their time to discuss the process, duration, the tests, and their respective roles during the evaluation. They further explained how they would observe our son for 3 hours in a play environment without us present. Paul and I would participate in two phases of the meeting, the initial interview and the final assessment, where each team member would review and discuss their findings and next steps.

Once the observations and reports were complete, the School Evaluation Team reconvened and met with Paul and me. Each team member reviewed their portion of the assessment and provided their conclusions. Their report indicated that our son had some developmental delay based on their observation and findings. Their conclusive diagnosis was Pervasive Developmental Disorder - Not Otherwise Specified (PDD-NOS). This diagnosis meant that Jamir had developmental concerns requiring additional support and related services within a school setting. Their next steps concluded that Jamir would benefit from an early childhood special education setting where he would receive support services. Those services included speech and language therapy, occupational therapy, music and art therapy, bus transportation to and from school, and periodic home visits.

As the intervention team continued to report their findings, Paul Sr. was devastated. Sitting next to him, I could feel his energy and body shift as he placed his head into his clasped hands while tears streamed down his face. As I attempted to comfort him by placing my hand on his shoulder, I was relieved to have this missing piece to the puzzle finally revealed. I finally had an answer that now made logical sense regarding my son's behaviors he had been displaying since he was six months old. As a parent, I knew that early intervention was vital. Now, equipped with a diagnosis, we could finally pursue the most appropriate measures to support ourselves to best support our son.

A few weeks later, Jamir's early childhood special education services began at the Meadowview School in Country Club Hills, Illinois. It was a great fit. With a committed and dedicated school team's support, Jamir started progressing. Jamir appeared so happy to be in his new school with his peers, and we looked forward to meeting the goals we collectively set for Jamir to attain each academic year. We also had terrific, related services we put in place outside the school district. A special thank you to Mr. Arnell Brady Sr., our son's speech and language pathologist, who worked wonderfully in supporting Jamir with speech services.

Jamir was fortunate in that he had two loving, supportive parents and a supportive extended family. PJ and his dad were like Mufasa and Simba from Lion King. They developed their own language, watched sports, and had a great father/son relationship. When Jamir was 7 years old, he began participating in Special Olympics, which was truly a game-changer. A special shout out to Mr. Victor Winston, the Special Therapeutic Recreational Coordinator at Bessemer Park, and the entire staff, who have always been a consistent extended family to ours. Paul and Victor ensured that PJ competed in various activities and PJ was always proud to show our family and friends the medals he won. I was proud to see his dad embrace and protect his son.

At age 22, Jamir aged out of his high school program. Shout out to the lovely staff at Kenwood Academy High School and Ray Graham Training Center High School, who supported Jamir with strategic and intentional growth. He thrived in these academic spaces and was part of the greater school community. We couldn't have found better educational programs for him. He even learned to speak Spanish and American Sign Language (ASL). Despite his concerns about developing epilepsy, Jamir had perfect attendance, and the students at Kenwood Academy looked out for my son.

Aging out of high school at 22.5, literally the day before his 23rd birthday, was one of the worst transitions for Jamir. This transition meant he lost his daily interaction and connection to peers (i.e., Best Buddies), his teachers, his schooling, and being part of a consistent regiment and routine he enjoyed and looked forward to most. Youth on the autism spectrum can be particularly regimented and function and adapt well when maintaining consistent structures in their daily scheduled lives. For Jamir and other children on the autism spectrum, this helps to keep them and their behaviors more balanced while supporting their overall functioning.

As a mom, I have always been proactive, thinking about the next steps for Jamir. This included constantly researching what I could provide or offer my son next. I was on this constant merry-go-round, never-ending carousel about, "What can I do for PJ?" As a parent of a youth or adolescent on the autism spectrum, I felt like I never did enough, and still, at times, I have questioned this. I am constantly thinking about his future. These looming questions consume my thoughts most hours, most days of the week. I spend hours upon hours looking for programs designed or created to cater to my son's needs.

Those that appeared or stated that they were "acceptance-friendly" or "inclusive" precisely indicated one of the typical buzzwords, saying that they served "special children," "children with disabilities," "Children on the autism spectrum," etc. I would seek those words out because it typically meant that my son may have a place or a program where he can participate, and I can breathe for just a moment. And when I wasn't researching any programs online, I would sit for hours and ponder what my son's future could or would look like. Questions such as, how will my son's adult life look like? Will he have or maintain a career? Will he find love or ever marry? Are children or grandchildren in our future? Who will look after and take care of my son when his father and I are deceased? Will he be safe, particularly as an African American male with limited expressive language? How does he navigate the police or anyone who could bring him harm? One of the saddest things I reflect on is that I had to teach my son to hold his hands upright when he hears the word "freeze," "stop," or "don't move!" I have cried every time I taught or reinforced this measure with him. It hurts my soul tremendously, but as a 6'3, and over 200lbs black male, he is a target for pain, and if black males who maintain and have language aren't able to protect themselves from such harm, what does this mean for Jamir. This, too, is our reality.

Social spaces like movie theaters or workout facilities with designated family washrooms are helpful. What restaurants are more optimal for us to attend? Are there better grocery stores that he can handle and more that can accept him if he is dealing with too many stimuli?

For example, the airport has been a space where an overabundance of stimulation occurs in the environment. Yes, traveling can be challenging, even for those not on the autism spectrum. However, as we travel, TSA and Southwest Airlines have been so gracious with my son and his needs. I am super thankful for their support, ensuring that any assistance or help I have requested has consistently been provided.

FUNdaMENTALs: The essential needs

Yes, I was that young mother who frantically ran out of the mall in tears when Jamir couldn't sit for that Christmas photo with Santa that many families take with their children. A special thanks to my mother! She remained inside the mall with Jamir while I made a mad dash to my car and boo-hoo'ed profusely. Yes, a few years later, we finally got his picture with Santa because we weren't going to be embarrassed for behavior we didn't control. Yes, I am the mother who sat in the audience and cried when she saw her son singing in his first and only school performance at Keller Regional Gifted. A special shout-out to his teacher Mrs. Roberta Albee. Jamir was on stage singing and rocking in the opposite direction of his peers, looking a lot like Ray Charles, but I was so emotionally proud of him that I could witness my son being part of the Christmas program. Yes, I was that screaming mom when my son ran up and down a mountain in Galena, Illinois, and won a gold medal in snowshoeing competition with the Special Olympics. A special shout-out to Coach Montoya Morgan, Liria Lee, and the Bessemer Bear Athletes. This is "our normal," and I have cherished every moment and memory shared.

As Jamir grew, I grew as a parent of a developing autistic (as some on the spectrum like to be referred to) child through puberty and adulthood. And just as parents of any child, we navigated through all the developmental milestones, maybe with more challenges, but we survived. In the past 10 years, I have come to realize that he is not much different than other young adults. I had to change my way of parenting as he matured; I still navigate how to change as his protector.

Therefore, I do not accept mediocrity or false promises made by individuals who say or indicate they'll get back to me. I have become increasingly adamant that the needs requested for my son are met with fidelity.

This may seem a unique approach as Jamir, and I are together for a lifetime. I mean, yeah, well, autism does socially and biologically lead to some unique neurological conditions that cause social and communication concerns. And yes, this reinforces a display of other behaviors and quirks, such as stimming, hand-flapping, squeezing his hands together, closing his eyes, and touching the walls between going through spaces such as the entrances and hallways. HOWEVER, like most other youth, his FUNdaMENTAL needs are much the same. He desires and seeks approval, loves to be loved and praised, plays sports, loves his iPad, enjoys puzzles and mathematics, plays UNO, listens to Bob Marley, recites lines from his favorite movies and television shows, and has crushes on pretty young ladies. Yes, PJ has his eyes on the girls; he is a big flirt. Just maybe, he commands more time, attention, and support than the average youth or adult. But did I mention he is clever and often uses his "DIS-ability" to get others to work and do things on his behalf? And he's funny, just like his dad!

As I now reflect, sometimes, my vigilant approach to try and "normalize" my son's behavior to such standards as defined by others served totally as the means to protect him. Like race, is "disability" juxtaposed with "ability" a social construction that needs dismantling? Hmmm!

My son exists in what I call "an autism realm." One in which he or I do not control or would even want to if we could. I respect the space in which my son exists. It puts me in the context of that John Travolta movie, "Boy in the Bubble". Autism is in a dimension like a deity (a quality) that cannot be physically seen or touched, but you know it's there. Through this autism realm, which I have come to acknowledge as a part of my son's makeup or existence, Jamir, more than any of us, knows what he needs and perhaps how he should acquire it. He allows you in when he wants to and blocks you out when he needs to. Jamir plays by his own set of rules, and on most days, he takes me and selective others along his journey, not the other way around. Jamir and I are genuinely one and the same: personality, demeanor, and love for the simple things in life. We're even born 5- days apart; my Christmas Eve, Eve Baby for sure. Jamir chose Paul and me to be his parents because he already knew we'd unconditionally love him and that we'd have his back. Jamir has been the one who has taught me personally the value of pure love and that living your best life is providing adequate care, patience, and service to others no matter what.

Your Superhero lives inside!
So, I STOPPED waiting for this Superhero...or in our case, I stopped looking for the "autism" specialist. Among the medical areas of dentistry, neurology, and pharmacology, across several schools he attended, the suburban swim program, the music ensemble, the art-based program, etc., I engaged in NORMALIZing my son's life with Autism as best as I could. His label of being autistic is a label with significant meaning for his entire life. However, as he exists within our family, he also belongs to the greater community, with everyday experiences and realities that shape his being. This rethinking has made a difference for my son and how we CHOOSE to navigate such spaces. Like many other supportive, caring parents, my job is to protect my son and help guide him as best as I can along the way. This is significant because I accepted my role as not only Jamir's mother but also a systems thinker and advocate for others on the spectrum and their caregivers. This role positioned me to align the world around him while aligning and equipping the world to include him too! Each opportunity that Jamir engages with the general public is an opportunity to teach others about him, Autism, and the possibilities that emerge from such engagement. Also, it was an open and ongoing invitation to model and teach others how to engage and or exist with individuals on the autism spectrum and other varying abilities. My Great-Grandma, Delessa Poindexter, used to say,

"Teach them how to treat you!" And this applies to what we have done. On October 27, 2017, at 7:17 pm, Jamir and I lost his father and best friend. Our son was with his father during his final moments. The transition of Paul Andre' Hutchins, # 67, with the Green Bay Packers Franchise was indeed a "Gentle Giant!" And though we still are grieving such a tremendous loss, we still feel his presence, grace, and energy. I make no decisions about our son without the guidance of his spirit. He loved our son, and I am grateful that my son knows just how much his father loved him. I have been charged with something greater than I could have ever imagined possible. Please stay tuned! And as Hutch would often say to us at home, "It's my turn to pick up and carry the ball...!"

In loving memory
Paul J. Hutchins

"Did you know that true love asks for nothing
Her acceptance is the way we pay
Did you know that life has given love a guarantee
To last through forever and another day...ALWAYS"
~Stevie Wonder 'As'

Biography

Nycole A. Buckner is an educational consultant, counselor, and mentor. She is passionate about life, mental health, and social justice. Her most precious commodity on this planet is her 27-year old son Paul Jamir "PJ" Hutchins, who has autism and epilepsy. He is the reason why she remains a staunch advocate in program development, research, and advocacy for persons diagnosed with ASD (autism spectrum disorder). She is actively involved with organizations that support youth and adults with autism and other special abilities. She volunteers with Special Olympics Illinois and Autism Speaks, which raises awareness and monies to support additional research for persons along the autism spectrum.

In addition to her many roles, she is in the process of developing an organization called Bleuprint LLC. This organization is dedicated to enhancing the lives of youth and young adults with Autism and other confounding special abilities. Bleuprint's motto is, "We don't just make dreams possible; we assist with bringing them to fruition!"

Nycole holds a Bachelor of Arts Degree in Psychology and African American Studies from the University of Illinois at Chicago and a Master of Arts Degree in Education from DePaul University. She is affiliated with the University of Chicago, where she has worked in several capacities for the Urban Education Institute. She is a member of Alpha Kappa Alpha, Sorority Inc. and is currently completing a Master of Arts Degree in Counseling Psychology.

Acknowledgments

I want to take this time and opportunity to say, "THANK YOU!" Thank you, God, for another day to get things in working order.

Thank you to all the people who have been there, held my hand, listened to my plea, or found something that supports me in supporting Jamir. I am forever grateful and appreciative of you.

To my immediate and loving family, my mother, Reneau A. Diallo, my Aunt Deborah A. Underwood, my siblings Erik J. Buckner and N'kechi Q. Hendrickson, and my nieces, the eldest set of twins Erika & Akire and my youngest set of twins nieces Zuri & Zoey and my Godmother Ann Moorehead; THANK YOU! Words cannot express what each of you mean to Pj and me. Thank you for ALWAYS being in our corner and having our back no matter what! We love you! To Aunt Sheila and Uncle Calvin Lane, we love you to pieces. Thank you for being an intricate part of our lives.

To our Bessemer Park family and staff, you already know what you mean in our hearts and soul. Thanks again, Mr. Victor A. Winson, Ms. Montoya Morgan, Ms. Liria Lee, Ms. Kenisha Harper, and Mr. Erie Ward. You will always be family to us!

A very special thank you to our close friends and their loved ones on the spectrum: Kafi & Aaron Patterson (Lawrence Moragne), Lisa Allseits (Patrick), Elaine Reeves-Haywood (Malcolm), Antoinette Newsome (David & Marcus), Stattina Horace (D'Andre Miller), Charlene Cutright (Cebastian Brown), Lillian Beatrice Tyler (Keith), Tiffany Alexander-Jones (Carmen) Denise Von Moore (Donese), Lorraine Langston (Devontae "Kool" Barton), Donna Hollis (Ryan), Felecia West-Brown (Jalen), Kimberly Ford (Kayla), Sandra Myrick (Clayton), Gina Cross (Nicole), Niki Buckner (Vincent), Brianna Lee, Anthony Walker and many, many other families that we are intricately connected. We have been on this ride graciously together!

Thank you to those women who stand with me and listen to all my crazy ideas and concepts while allowing me to dream freely. Thank you, Tracy Lynn Cox (TLC), Sharonda Marchelle Kimbrough, Deidre Jordan, Medea Brooks, Diamond Brown, Stacy Joann Williams, Angela Celeste Vernadob. I cannot thank each of you enough for being ultra-fantastic women and sisters in this walk of life.

Last and certainly not least, Thank YOU to this incredible group of contributors, the Exceptional Mothers and professionals who not only found the courage to share our stories but yielded the tenacity to fight and advocate on behalf of our children, despite the obstacles endured. This journey has indeed been a labor of love. Thank you, Khadija Ali, for all you have done in bringing this collaboration together.
Much love, Sis!

The Extraordinary Mr. Miles

Everyone knew I was extremely excited when I became pregnant with my second child, Miles. Since my first child was born in 1996, I was looking forward to having another baby. My first son, Malcolm, was born with cleft palate and micrognathia. Micrognathia is a condition in which a child is born with a very small lower jaw. His condition required constant monitoring from pediatric surgeons, developmental pediatricians; ear, nose ,and throat doctors, and several other specialists.

It was a constant struggle to keep him healthy but he made it through his surgeries for the cleft palate with few complications. He also grew out of the micrognathia so we did not have to have any corrective surgeries or therapies for that. Needless to say, I was very worried that I would have to go through this again. And so, for these reasons, I wanted to be more cautious with this child.

While I was pregnant, I had several ultrasounds, lab tests, and all of the blood work that you could possibly imagine. All seemed well, according to the doctors and specialists. The only issue I had with my pregnancy with Miles was my awful morning sickness and nausea. It was the worst! I had morning sickness with Malcolm, but nothing like this. With Malcolm, it lasted for only 3 months. With Miles, I could barely eat and I felt like I was starving.

I couldn't eat crackers or pretzels to settle my stomach. Not even ginger ale or fresh ginger would work. Feeling desperate, I purchased pressure point bracelets to quell the symptoms and give me some relief. Sadly, that didn't work either. What a waste of money! I was so frustrated.

I was not able to sleep. Smells, the motion of the car, the sight of raw meat;

As a last resort, I went back to my doctor and talked to him about it again. Surprisingly, he actually listened to me and prescribed Zofran instead of dismissing me like he did the first time. Zofran is an anti-nausea medication generally prescribed to cancer patients. My mother, a cancer survivor, used Zofran to increase her appetite. So, I trusted my doctor and assumed it would be safe.

My other issue was how big he was getting. Before he was born, he was so heavy. I could barely carry him. I wasn't eating, but he was huge! His size made it hard for me to walk because he was laying on my sciatic nerve. I had never been so uncomfortable in my entire life.

When he was born, in July of 2004, he weighed eight pounds, and eight ounces. The size may not seem like a big deal to others, but to someone who was barely eating and sleeping; and I was small framed to boot, it was painful. Regardless of this, I was still elated to be having another baby.

When he was born, just like his brother, Malcolm, he didn't cry right away. I wasn't overly concerned until the doctor said he wasn't moving one of his arms. I was just so happy to be done with the birthing process and very excited to have my baby finally born that nothing bothered me initially. Suddenly and without a word, the nurse whisked my baby out of the room. Just as suddenly, I was concerned because I never had the chance to hold him. What was going on? Those first few moments right after birth are very important to both the mother and the new baby. I felt completely cheated out of that moment.

What made it even worse, they refused to let me see him for three whole hours. What an agonizing three hours! No one had spoken to me, no one checked on me, and no one gave me any updates. It was absolute agony not knowing what was going on with my son.

Finally, he was brought to me. They told me his shoulder issue had been resolved and he was in great shape. Finally, I was able to kiss and cradle my baby. I had been waiting for this moment for months. The memories of backaches, nausea, and exhaustion faded away as I looked at my handsome little boy and closely examined every inch of him. Once I was satisfied that everything was fine, I immediately put him to my breast and my milk came down in record time. We were both quite content. His first day of nursing was a clear indication of what a great appetite he would have– to this day, that young man can EAT!

All was well in my world since now everything was well in his. The relief and contentment in my heart was a soothing balm and helped me forget the previous hours.

My husband and I were somewhat concerned about Miles when we realized he was screaming his way through many nights. Most of the time, his crying lasted for 3 to 4 hours a night and we were told this was a normal thing. So, we worked through it for three months and believed that he was just being colicky.

Miles seemed to be on time with getting teeth, eating solids and crawling and his growth was off the charts. Then, at about age 4...we noticed a few odd things. It seemed as though his development came to a halt and he was picking up some strange habits.

He started sitting really close to the television. He wasn't very interested in talking. He didn't seem to hear us when we were talking to him. He liked wearing only certain outfits and they had to be tight to his skin. On the other hand, he hated wearing shoes and the kid who used to love baths was suddenly afraid of the water?!

Shortly after I noticed changes at home, the director of his daycare pulled me aside to talk about Miles' development. She noticed that he didn't seem to be picking up things like some of the other children. For example, he was not reading simple words; and he was not learning his letters or his numbers.

The director also noticed that his social skills were suffering. Since he didn't communicate or understand as well as the other children, Miles was isolating himself and being teased by his schoolmates. He also had some unique habits - like his absolute refusal to wear shoes every day. She recommended testing by the local school district as a starting point to understand what was happening with my baby boy.

Feeling extremely alarmed, I made an appointment with the district's testing center. Several hours later, I received good news and bad news: his hearing problem was due to the need for ear tubes and he needed glasses. I was relieved to know that these were issues that I was already familiar with and had dealt with before when his older brother was small.

After I learned about him needing glasses and ear tubes, he was given more diagnoses. I was told he was developmentally delayed and had sensory processing disorder. This explained why he liked to wear certain clothing and had a fear of water. He needed to feel certain textures to be comfortable. The tight clothes gave him a sense of security and the feeling of water was just weird to him.

He also had cognitive speech problems. It was recommended that he receive occupational therapy to refine his motor skills and speech therapy for his stuttering. He was diagnosed with a non-specific learning disability that was later specified when he was in middle school.

They threw so much at me that day. I was completely frozen for the rest of the afternoon; trying to digest it all. Essentially, he was going to need a lot of support in school.

Thinking back, I wonder if the medicine (Zofran) had a negative effect on him. I truly wonder.

Based on the testing center's recommendation, I enrolled him in Exceptional Student Education (ESE) PreK for the summer. He absolutely thrived in his classes. He made so much progress that summer and he was happy. It was evident that this was the kind of support he needed all along.

When he started kindergarten, I thought he would receive the same support he received in the summer. Oh boy, that wasn't true at all!

Back then, I did not understand the concept of push-ins. A push-in is when the teacher who works with exceptional students comes to (or pushes into) the regular education class to assist the special education student with school work or class participation. On occasion, the teacher will pull the student out of the class to work one on one with the student on an individualized activity.

In my opinion, he was not getting the constant support and supervision he needed. Miles was in a regular class with 24 other students. He received support from Exceptional Education teachers and was pulled out of his classes for speech therapy and occupational therapy. In addition to those services, he had a (push-in)teacher sit with him in class for perhaps an hour a day.

For example, the teacher would have a fun activity for the class and he would be excited to participate. Then, here comes the push-in teacher or he would be pulled out of class for speech or OT. It made him realize that he was being left out of things because of the support he needed. He wasn't happy about that at all. He wanted to do what all of the other children were doing. He didn't like being singled out either. I kept assuring him that he needed this help and he began to accept it.

Thinking back...how was this supposed to help him learn? I suppose it did help him learn some things, in a way. It made him understand (that) he was different from other children. It was easy for him to understand why speech therapy was necessary but he did not think it was fair to be pulled out of class while everyone else was having fun. These experiences taught him not so much about academics as much as it taught him about life.

When Miles reached middle school, everything changed for him. He was forced to learn to change classes essentially on his own. He had six different teachers, and none of them had the time to help a student who was struggling like Miles was. His grades began to drop until he was failing almost every class. I kept communication open with each of his teachers to see what we could do to help. Three or four of them tried to work with, while the others could have cared less. To these teachers, he was failing and that wasn't their fault in the slightest bit. One of them rarely responded to my emails or phone calls. When she did, she had nothing to contribute to the conversation. Her attitude was basically, "Not my fault. I'm doing my job. He needs to do his and you need to do yours."

None of them had the time to help him, and I had to make myself understand that. After a semester of Miles and I both being upset about his grades, I started doing some research. Yes, he had a learning disability, but was it definable? I wished several times that my husband would have been still alive because I felt he would have known what to do right away. But it was just me and no one could offer me any assistance. After doing some internet searches and reading, I decided to have Miles tested for autism. Many of his "peculiarities" (speaking with little inflection in his voice, not making eye contact, not liking being too hot or over dressed) pointed to that diagnosis, so I pressed the school to get him tested. They did a few weeks of testing and even came to our home and talked to me for a couple of hours. I hated all of the questions and testing, but I felt in my heart that this was how I was going to get some answers. I just wanted to help my sweet boy.

I was called to the school for a meeting. I was used to this because every year I had to have an IEP (Individualized Educational Plan) meeting with his teachers, the principal, staffing specialist, and therapists to discuss his progress. We also discussed and put together a plan for the fall. This meeting was different. I walked into the room and there had to be about 10 people there, all looking expectantly at me. IEP meetings always made me a bit nervous, but this was a bit overwhelming! I remembered why I was there and hid my true feelings.

When I sat down, the people in the room introduced themselves. Then I was given several reports about Miles, completed by most of the people in that room. Based on all of the reports and observations made by the meeting participants, Miles had intellectual disability, with an IQ of 70. They explained what that meant: he would need specialized classes more suited to how he learned. These classes were self-contained and had specially trained teachers.

He would have the same basic curriculum as non-differently abled students but modified for his ability. After listening to everything that was said, I was actually relieved to know there was a name for Miles' learning disability and that there was assistance in place to help him.

I gave permission for him to be in those classes and have transportation to and from school catered to his needs. To be honest, it all had not sunk in yet. I didn't digest everything until later at home.

When I was ready, I took out all of the reports and forms and read them from beginning to end. I learned that intellectual disability was a "PC" term for "mental retardation." My sweet boy was "retarded!?" How can that be? How did that happen? What kind of life would he have? I cried for a long time as I read and looked up various terms on the internet. How in the world was I supposed to cope with this by myself?

After that bout of grief and self-pity, I straightened up. Miles had always been this way. He hadn't changed. There was just a name to how his mind works now. Having that name helped me understand how to help him. That was the entire point of this exercise, wasn't it? I learned everything I could about intellectual disability. I realized that there are some things that he may never do, like drive or live on his own. But there is plenty he can do and the best thing I could do is help him maximize what he can do.

The new classes, called Access Points, were just what he needed. The classes were small and all of the students had some kind of disability. The teachers and teacher's aides were trained in how to work with these students. They used plenty of patience and even more encouragement. The Access Points teachers were with the students all day long and even made sure they got to the cafeteria or to a general education class, such as Art or Music. I noticed a change almost immediately in Miles. I began to see a new confidence in him I hadn't really seen before. Finally, he was getting the attention he needed in school and was able to learn at his own pace with the modified curriculum. With the help of his new classes, his grades improved significantly. He even made the honor roll several times between the seventh grade and eleventh grade! I was so proud of him. He was succeeding and thriving... like I knew that he could.

Miles Extraordinaire

Ever since he was born and every minute of his life, Miles has been an extraordinary human being. I have already spoken about his beginnings and the obstacles he faced. However, I haven't talked about who and what he is. Miles is the embodiment of his father's heart. My husband was a big, sometimes very gruff man who hid a kind and loving soul underneath that angry-looking exterior. Miles is all of that kindness and love inside and out. I have never met a single person who didn't love him. He is a big bear of a young man, but he has the gentlest soul I have ever seen. He cares about everyone. Can you imagine that? A child who was misunderstood as much as he has been isn't bitter or angry. He is as pure a person as I have ever met.

Miles was still very young when my husband got sick. When my husband would come home from one of his many hospital stays and had to sleep in a hospital bed in the living room, Miles asked to sleep on the couch so his dad wouldn't be alone. My son often helped me care for Tony, feeding him dinner and gathering medical supplies so that I could give my husband his medications or tend to his personal needs. When Tony died, I was devastated. But the first thing Miles said to me was "Dad is still with us, Mom." He's repeated that to me when I would have rough days stewing in my grief and pain. I also believe his father speaks to me through him. One of Tony's phrases he would say to me is "I'm with you all the way." On a tough day at work then coming home to argue again with my oldest, Miles said to me, "Dad is with you all the way. Don't forget." My eyes got huge and I asked him "What did you say? What was that?" Miles had no idea what I was asking him and was not able to repeat the phrase.

Miles is not perfect. He's stubborn and can be very single-minded. If I don't answer him right away about something, he digs in and keeps asking until I tell him. His exceptionalities on occasion can make everyday living difficult. Being afraid of bad weather is typical for many people, but Miles is absolutely terrified of storms and will constantly ask me how hard it is going to rain and if I know the exact time it will stop. If I don't say something, I am in for a day of persistent questions until he is satisfied with what I tell him. He's afraid of dogs, all dogs, no matter what size. So afraid in fact that he will grab my arm and try to drag me while he runs! To the outside world, some of the things he does are plain weird. To me, he is just Miles.

My extraordinary Mr. Miles.

Biography

Cheryl Barnes was born in Atlanta, Georgia and after several moves with her family, settled in Indianapolis, Indiana. She attended college at Indiana University Bloomington, where she majored in Public and Environmental Affairs Management. While she attended college, she laid eyes on Martin "Tony" Barnes and was completely lost. They became inseparable and were married on December 24th, 1991. After five years of marriage, their first son, Malcolm, was born on New Year's Eve, 1996. After Tony obtained his Master's Degree in Social Work in 2002, the family moved to Orlando, Florida. Tony worked as a counselor, while Cheryl got her dream job working at Walt Disney World. Two years later, their second son, Miles, was born in July 2004. A year after Miles was born, Cheryl left Disney and took a job as the accounting supervisor at a property management company. Everything seemed to be going well for the family and Cheryl made plans to attend nursing school. However, in July 2011, Tony was diagnosed with end stage renal failure caused by lupus. For the next three years, Cheryl cared for her husband while working and taking care of their sons. Tony's health deteriorated, as a result of several complications, until he passed away on August 29, 2014. Thus, began her new journey as a widow and single parent.

Cheryl was devastated by the loss of her beloved Tony. She began writing as a way to work through her grief. At first, writing was only something she did only for herself. But, being encouraged by others, she began publishing her blog, "Widowness and Light." She has worked for six years in accounting at a property management company. She has been in her current position as a Dedicated Service Coordinator in Financial Reporting since January 2022.
Her hobbies are reading, attending Orlando Magic games, yoga, seeing movies with her son, Miles, jewelry-making, going to the beach, and just chilling with her boys.

Acknowledgments

It's hard to have a special needs child and it's even harder to find people who understand and want to support you as you raise and advocate for that child. It's even rarer to find those who love him as much as you do. But the people on this list do (did) and that means more than anything else.

These people were able to offer me and Mr. Miles immeasurable support as he grew and I need them to know
 how much they mean to us:

My mother, Sandra Blackburn and my sister/"ace", Denise Blackburn. They have always been there for me when I needed someone to listen to my frustrations, help me understand, and offer wisdom when I need it. Best of all, they accept my child for who he is and for where he is at the moment. To them, he's just Miles.

Martin Anthony "Tony" Barnes, (dec) - my wonderful late husband. I have always felt that Miles was a gift Tony left me with and I will always thank him for that. Miles is Tony's mini-me in so many ways, and I know that Tony would be proud of Miles and
how far he has come.

Holli Findley (dec) - Miles' daycare director who treated every child just like they were her own. She helped me understand that my child wasn't like others and that it was okay that he wasn't.

Davi Budnik, Vista Lakes Elementary - Miles' 5th-grade teacher. The first teacher to truly understand how special Miles is.

Christopher Hall, Lake Nona Middle School - Miles' 6th-grade math teacher. The second teacher who understood Miles and truly wanted to help.

Marcus Taunton and Fernando Colon - two teachers who were wonderful male influences for Miles.

Jayne Schuler - my best friend of forty years who loves Miles and spoils him like he deserves to be.

My co worker/friends - Natalie Younger, Jerilyn Melendez and Mama Sue Young. Jerilyn and Natalie only really know Miles through me and they love him just as much as I do. That means so much to me. Jerilyn always makes sure he gets his macaroni and cheese and chicken nuggets! Mama Sue brings treats to us at work and never forgets to give me something special for Miles.

UNEXPECTED BLESSING

Na'Sion (pronounced Nation) was born on July 18, 2002. According to his medical records, he took his first gasp of air at 11 minutes old. After he was born, the doctors and staff, who were with me during delivery, crowded into my hospital room. I was told my baby would be a vegetable for the rest of his life and that he would not be able to walk, talk or move on his own.

Four days after hearing this life-changing news and giving birth, I was discharged from the hospital. It was a very difficult time for me and I was not in a good place. While my son stayed in the NICU, I traveled back and forth to visit him. Every day, I would either touch him, hold him, talk to him, or sing to him. Or sometimes, I would cry.

His brain had been deprived of oxygen, so it was predicted that he would need a breathing tube and a feeding tube for his entire life. It was suggested that if he survived, he would probably stay in the hospital for months and maybe for years. Against all odds, Na"Sion overcame his obstacles and was out of the hospital in 17 days. Miraculously, his hospital stay did not take several weeks, months or years and he was discharged on August 3, 2002, my 24th born day.

The first day we brought him home was also the first day that he opened his eyes. After hearing me say, "This is your home and we are your family", Na'Sion finally opened his eyes. I cried tears of joy and relief because it was unclear when or if he would ever open his eyes. It felt like he chose to wait until he left the hospital to see his family. I received two miracles on my birthday. My baby opened his eyes for the first time and he left the hospital long before expected.

Now that we were finally home, I was able to do things for him that I could not do when he was in the incubator. The simple act of changing my baby's diaper was extremely difficult and stressful. I had to hold his legs open with my arms while putting on his diaper.

His arms and legs were so tight that dressing him had me in tears daily. I was puzzled since I did not change his diaper or dress him in the NICU. Sometimes, I was afraid to move him because I didn't want to hurt him.

If I had been given the opportunity to have some of these experiences in the hospital, I would have asked more questions and felt more prepared to help Na'Sion. I felt like my interaction with him was extremely limited in the hospital and the medical staff could have been much more informative and supportive. They could have given me a diagnosis for him and a treatment plan. At the very least, there should have been a social worker to help me with navigating future medical care.

All of this motivated me to do some research online and find out what could be the cause. Back then, information was not as easy to find as it is today. Keep in mind, this was 2002 and the internet was in its very early stages and was nothing like it is today. There was no Google search engine. The only options were Ask Jeeves and Yahoo Search. Imagine that doing research meant using my home phone line to get a dial-up connection to America Online (AOL).

The first thing I researched was key terms like, "babies having stiff limbs or appendages". Based on my research, I diagnosed him with cerebral palsy. Then, I immediately scheduled an appointment to share my findings with his pediatrician. After the exam, he agreed that I was correct. Eight months after he was born, in April 2003, I received Na'Sion's spastic quadriplegic cerebral palsy diagnosis. The diagnosis was a turning point for me and a confirmation. I knew that something was going on with my child and it was not just in my head.

Tears of relief rolled down my face. Yes, I was relieved because now we knew exactly what was wrong with our baby, but I was so angry that he would be in a wheelchair and have other special needs. Along with being angry,

I was grief-stricken and devastated. Digesting the loss of knowing he could never have a normal childhood was heartbreaking. For the rest of his life, I would be his caregiver; and eventually, his legal guardian. All of this was very overwhelming and it was all very devastating for me. I was only 23 years old at the time, and there was so much responsibility placed on me.

On the other hand, it was very reassuring to hear the doctor's confirmation of my research. Now, I felt more encouraged and empowered to be Na'Sion's number one advocate. With all that I was processing as a young mother, I knew in my heart that I would do everything in my power to ensure that my son would have the best quality of life that could be provided for him.

After that day, we started on the next part of our journey. I was instructed to apply for Social Security Income. After going through the process, Na'Sion was awarded SSI. Until he was of school-age, we received in-home support through Early Intervention Services. From that point, different programs and resources became available. Since he was 4 years old, Easter Seals has been providing him with services. Now, he is on their waiting list to restart physical therapy. From all of these experiences, I learned that resources in Pennsylvania are great for special needs children. We are still utilizing some of these programs today. Currently, we are working with SAM (Service Access Management) and AIM (Abilities In Motion) for respite care and extra support. I am very grateful for having access to these invaluable resources as he transitions into manhood.

Reflecting back on those early years, I felt like I was going through the motions as I took care of my boys. I did not have the luxury of slowing down to fully take care of myself or to understand how to cope with my postpartum depression. With all of the responsibilities of raising my sons and keeping a routine, I functioned like a robot. While I was coping with my 3 other sons and Na'Sion's special needs, life was throwing me another curve ball. My mom was battling Breast Cancer.

In March of 2007, she passed away. When my mother passed, I realized that I had been depressed and dealing with postpartum for years. Coping with the grief and the impact of everything else in my life left me in an extremely dark place. I did not want to be around my family nor did I want to be sociable. I stopped attending family functions and that left me feeling very lonely because of my self-imposed isolation.

I was avoiding any level of commitment because of all the responsibilities placed on me as a 24 year old mother. I stopped wanting to be touched and hugged. I had no desire for physical contact from anyone; not even my husband and our children. This new found feeling put a big strain on our relationship because he did not understand. Feeling overwhelmed and being young, while working on having a "serious adult" relationship with their father...all of it came crashing down on me.

Life was moving by at such a fast pace and everything was coming at me from all directions. At the time, I did not realize it, but I was in shock about everything that was happening. Honestly, I was on autopilot, not truly grasping everything or fully embracing my new reality. I felt so numb to everything. The uncertainty left me with a sense of confusion. There was so much to think about and so much to do.

Having felt like I was having a mental breakdown, with all of life's happenings, I had thoughts about committing myself into a mental hospital. Instead of displacing myself by separating myself from my family, I went to a therapist and was prescribed Paxil. The medication did not work for me. It made me feel like a zombie. So, I stopped taking it.

Even though the medication did not work, I gained a very valuable lesson from the therapist. There was a written exercise for me to do at home that really helped me. She told me to write down everything that I was in control of in my life. At that moment, when I started to think about it, I realized that I was not in control of anything! That was a BIG AHA MOMENT for me. This acceptance brought me so much inner peace and taught me how to simply be in the moment while moving through life from day to day.

As I reflect on all the events, it makes sense that I was so numb and operating in survival mode. After all, I had been through so much. That time gave me a chance to see how important communication is and how to stand strong in the midst of life's challenges. Now, I see relationships and communication in a whole new light. Listening to others with compassion is an integral part of building trust and healthy relationships.

I didn't know how difficult it would be: mentally, physically, spiritually, and emotionally but I have grown so much from being a mother. The skill of being resilient has been a blessing. Resilience has given me the capability to know how to cope with personal challenges and family changes. Through it all, I have learned to have more respect and appreciation for life's journey. I am aware that all of my experiences can positively affect every area of my life, if I allow it.

Throughout all of my experiences, I know I have been through all of the 7 stages of grief. The anger for the hospital's negligence is almost gone; but the hurt still lingers for the life Na'Sion would have had. He will never know what it is like to stand up, learn to walk, go down a flight of stairs, run, play outside with his brothers, or ride a bike. Nor did he have the opportunity to create memories like the average teenager who played sports, went to school dances, or hung out with friends at the arcade.

Looking back at that time, I had so many questions and so many thoughts about the things that I thought Na'Sion would never do... Would he be able to work? How hard would it be for him to get a good job? Would he get married and have children? Back then, there were so many unknown obstacles and so many unanswered questions. In the midst of all of these circumstances, he overcame barriers and learned to thrive.

My bud is older now. He graduated from high school in 2021. He receives an outpouring of support and resources from the school and other programs. Currently, he has been doing odd jobs working in the community and he has waivers to receive other services to help him transition into adulthood.

One of the many lessons I have learned from my son is that it is okay to be alone. He stays at home and keeps himself occupied. Actually, he would not have it any other way. He enjoys going out, but he is content with staying home. That is another lesson that I have learned from him. Being okay with yourself will help bring balance and help you tap into your inner zen.

He values the little things in life and is a perfect example of how we all should value the little things in life, too. There is so much that we take for granted. Walking up the stairs, pulling up our pants, using our hands to hold a washcloth to wash our bodies; or the act of simply rotating our ankles. These are some of the things we don't always notice, appreciate or even stop to think about while we are in motion.

From the time he could sit up until he was around 13 years old, he had physical therapy. From all of the therapy and stretching, Na'Sion's tailbone started to protrude outward and form a tail below his lower back. Learning the hard way that he would never be able to fully stand up and walk because of the tightness that goes down his body was hard to bear. It helped me see that it was our need for him to walk and not his wanting to walk that had him in physical therapy. We learned to be okay with it and accept that he would be in a wheelchair. He is content and at peace with the way things are and just wants to live his life. So, we started to embrace his reality with gratitude.

One of the many valuable lessons that I learned was that staying calm throughout any situation is the best practice. One example is when I found out that I could influence the outcome of his seizures by how calm I remained throughout an episode. As long as I stayed calm, then he was calm, too. That's when I realized that he fed off of my energy from the womb and continues to do so even now.

As mothers we try to be so strong, not realizing that our children have an emotional connection to us. I'm not sure that all mothers realize this. Even though I had other children, I didn't realize how much my energy could affect my children until I learned this lesson from Na'Sion.

The most impactful thing I learned as his mom was that he was actually addicted to the medicine prescribed to him for his seizures. He took that medicine from the time he was born until he was 13 years old. At his last neurologist appointment, I requested he have another test, called an EEG, to check his brain's electrical signals for seizures and there was no activity seen.

From that time, we started to wean him off the phenobarbital. That experience made me pay more attention to my family's health and ask more questions. Now, it has been 8 years since he has been off medication and he is as healthy as a bull!

Around 2008, I noticed a significant change in my attitude about life. Being in a positive and productive state of mind was my mission. My personal goals shifted. I started taking better care of myself. I read self-help books and learned about the power of manifestation. I began the process of rediscovering myself and embracing my authentic self.

Honestly, with all of life's challenges, I had to start exercising. Once I started exercising regularly, I found that release I was looking for and I started to heal. Exercise is my therapy. It has helped me to do the hard things for Na'Sion that he could not do for himself. I noticed that my energy level and my stamina increased. With more strength and endurance, my capability to lift him into his wheelchair, bathe him, help him get dressed; and be there for him mentally, amongst other things, improved.

Since we began this journey, the ability to have movement is so much more appreciated. Knowing the things that I can do that Na'Sion can not, gives me a new perspective and a whole new level of appreciation. Now that he is older, I have more freedom. So, I use my love of fitness to help other mothers appreciate their use of movement through exercise, too.

During high school, I was interested in totally different things. When I started college, I wanted a career in the field of Criminal Justice. I completed 2 semesters and had to stop because of no childcare. Then, I became an Independent Scentsy Consultant in September of 2011. I chose this career path to be more hands on with Na'Sion and his special needs. I love working with Scentsy and my love of aromatherapy and candles has been a bonus to compliment my decision. And to this day, I have never regretted my choice.

Currently, I have new career goals. Investing time into my passions has given me great joy and clarity around my purpose. I am working my way back to being a SPIN Instructor and a Beachbody Coach. I have been taking Voice Acting lessons and successfully recorded my first demo in May. And as a new Motivational Speaker, my first public speaking event was in June 2022.

Using my voice to inspire the world by sharing my stories and my love of reading is a passion that I am now rekindling. Once I released old limiting beliefs, I tapped into the interests and passions that I neglected in the past. One of my most recent breakthroughs was that I proudly rang the bell for my last chemotherapy and radiation treatments this past year. I won my battle with Breast Cancer!

Thinking back on everything, I realize that Na'Sion has made living in love and in light a priority for our family. We laugh more and we value the simple things in life more than we did before Na'Sion came into our lives. He has made us all see that when we appreciate the little things like simply being alive, life is much better.

We practice living without judgment and without indoctrinations. We are journeying through life, with a smile on our faces, having compassion for all, enjoying life: one day at a time. My resilient warrior, Na'Sion, is a light to whomever he meets. I aim to be a light to all I encounter by doing the things I love and sharing my light because of his influence.

My son is an angel and such a happy young man. He is my favorite human and is the light of our family. To this day, he amazes his doctors. They are literally dumbfounded by his progress and his accomplishments. It is a privilege and pure joy to be his mother and such an honor to guide him on his life journey.

Biography

Angela Williams is a native of Harford County, Maryland. She currently resides in Hamburg, Pennsylvania. She is the loving mother of four sons (ages 25, 23, 21, and 19), and a 3 year old Yorkie fur daughter. In 2002, she birthed an angel, who took his first gasp of air at eleven minutes old. His name is Na'Sion Seven and he is the "greatest uniter of love", as she calls him. Na'Sion, her youngest son, was diagnosed with spastic quadriplegia cerebral palsy in 2003. This major life change shaped her decision to be a work from home mom for the last twenty years. As a work from home mom, Angela advocates and encourages her son to know that the word "CAN'T" is definitely not an option; especially when it comes to expressing himself and doing what he wants.

For the past 10 years, she has been an Independent Scentsy Consultant. She started on her fitness journey in 2008. In 2013, her journey sparked a love for SPIN. As a result, she took it to the next level, and for the last 7 years, has been a Certified SPIN Instructor. Angela's most recent accomplishment in the world of health and fitness is becoming a Beachbody Coach in 2019. Everyday she works at inspiring others by holding herself accountable for getting in movement.

Embarking on a new journey and creating a new chapter in her life, Angela took her passion for inspiring people to another level in 2022. This led her to become a Resilience Coach and she completed her first public speaking event in June. After completing six months of Voice Acting lessons, her first demo was recorded in May. Honoring her own voice by using it to motivate others, Angela has found her passions!

Angela's life exemplifies victory and perseverance. She continues to show proof of that on her journey. During this last year, after completing chemotherapy and radiation, she proudly rang the bell to share that she was victorious in her fight. Angela won her battle against Breast Cancer and looks forward to new beginnings!

You can follow her on social media: **@awresiliencecoach** and **@todays_vibe4.0** on Instagram, **Today's Vibe** on YouTube, and her Facebook VIP Group- **Vibe's Goodies Lounge.** For more information on Scentsy you can visit **https://smellvibes.scentsy.us**

Acknowledgments

First, giving honor to God, my ancestors, and guides as they help me in life. Let me start by saying how very grateful I am for my four young men I've been blessed to have birthed. Kai, Curtis, NuBorn and Na'Sion; my buds. They have shaped my life into a journey of lessons on being a good human. I thank them with my whole heart and appreciate their understanding. I want to thank my Pop Pop for always being there when I need him even when I don't ask. Big thank you to my big sister Katrice for her support and understanding as I navigate family relationships. I would like to thank each and every person who has ever shared their knowledge or helped me grow mentally, physically, emotionally, or spiritually. Thank you, the reader, for taking the time to read my chapter. Lastly, I'd like to thank my husband Curtis for knowing a good thing. Twenty-Four years of learning life individually and with each other through good times and bad times. May we continue to build and destroy as necessary as we rebuild our relationship foundation.

My daughter has been one of my greatest teachers. On August 31, 1999 at 6:38 am, Qismah Amatullah-Azim arrived on the planet. In fact, I almost delivered her at home because my midwife did not think I was in active labor. Before going to bed and against the advice of my midwife, I drank a bottle of castor oil mixed with Sprite to bring on my labor. Shortly afterwards, I woke up because I quickly went into labor. "Goose" was born about 30 minutes after we arrived at the hospital. She came so quickly that I had to glance at the clock. As a mother of 3 children already, I expected a long labor like my previous birth experiences. I almost could not believe that she had arrived so fast!

Qismah was about two weeks overdue. When she came out, her fingernails were long and her skin was shedding due to being 'overcooked'. I was so relieved and paid attention to nothing else other than the fact that she was here and healthy. This was my child, my beautiful baby girl. Those first few precious moments were so priceless. Little did her father and I know that our world would be turned upside down and changed forever.

The next morning, the pediatrician came in to do the usual wellness baby check up. He spoke to both my husband and me and left to do the assessment. I remember thinking he was taking an unusually long time to return and give us the thumbs up. When he walked into the room, he had his head down and nervously started to share that there were some things he noticed about Qismah that were not the norm. As he spoke, all I heard was womp, womp, womp, like the teacher from Charlie Brown. My mind went blank and I remember my husband saying, 'wait! WAIT! What are you saying?' I started to cry as the pediatrician continued on, telling us that Qismah's ears were lower than most babies ears were, that she had a big space in between her big and second toe and that she had low muscle tone all over her body. He told us that he suspected that she had Down syndrome but genetic testing would confirm it and that it would take several weeks for the results.

One positive thing I can say about the experience was his impeccable bedside manner. He showed compassion for our devastation and shock. I realized that his initial nervousness was a reflection of his concern. After all, how are you supposed to deliver devastating news to unsuspecting parents? Once he left the room, all I wanted to do was hold my baby. I asked my husband, "What are we going to do?". He simply replied, 'Take care of her'.

Since I had a normal delivery, we were released from the hospital in the standard 48 hour window. While I struggled to make sense of it all; I had three other little ones at home who needed me. I cried for two weeks straight. In the shower. In the wee hours of the morning. I cried on my way back from dropping off my older children at school. I cried for the future I had imagined her having that now I wasn't so sure she would.

It felt like my baby had passed away. What would her future be like? This question and many more raced through my mind day and night. My husband helped out with feedings and diaper changes as much as he could. Then after two weeks, he returned to work. Now, most of the time, I was at home alone with my precious baby.

One thing I knew: she was MY BABY!. At the end of the day, she still needed me to feed her, change her and hold her. I prayed over her every chance I had. If I was giving her a bath, I would pray a silent prayer over her. I whispered in her ear and told her how loved she was and how amazing she was. I was taking care of her the best way I knew how; the same way I cared for my other children. Yet, she frequently had respiratory infections and trouble waking up for her feedings. I kept a strict schedule of feedings and attempted to exclusively breastfeed her. According to the doctors, she was not gaining enough weight. So, eventually, I supplemented my breast milk with formula.

Instinctively, I knew there had to be information somewhere for parents of children with Down syndrome. This was before we had the internet at our fingertips like we do now. So, I had to go to the bookstore and find books. I found three books that helped tremendously. I brought them home and read until I had a thorough understanding of Down syndrome. I learned that despite the challenges, people with this chromosomal disorder could possibly face, they went on to lead long, full lives. Finding out that my daughter had a chance at life shifted my perspective and I set out to educate her doctors on what I had learned.

Her pediatrician was kind and took care of Qismah when I brought her in for various well and sick visits. However, her knowledge of specific tests and growth charts for babies with Down syndrome was very limited. Despite her attentiveness, I was extremely shocked that she had very little medical knowledge in this area. For example, Qismah scored low on the growth chart for typical children at each doctor visit until I brought in the growth chart specifically for babies with Down syndrome. Once her doctor reconfigured her weight on the new chart, she weighed in 'normal'. I requested every medical diagnostic test according to the suggestions in the books I'd read. We also signed her up for the early intervention program in our county. She received speech, occupational and physical therapy from birth to three years old. She excelled in every therapy and it gave my husband and I confidence that our daughter would live well and thrive.

(Back then doctors were not very educated about Down syndrome and my visits to the Judy Center made a great impression on me. At this practice, it was such a large contrast from our normal pediatrician. They knew EVERYTHING about it; what tests we needed, statistics, current research, etc).

Our family unit became closer as a result of Qismah's birth. My husband became an advocate for our daughter and attended as many therapy sessions as I did. Our other children pitched in and learned ways to incorporate her therapy lessons into any playtime they had with their younger sister. She was able to learn how to talk and walk at the appropriate age because of her siblings. We all banded together and showered her with love, laughter and hugs. Being born into a large family turned out to be an unexpected blessing for Qismah. She was able to learn how to talk and walk at the appropriate age because of her siblings.

Life began to level out and our family life returned to some normalcy. I started networking and meeting other parents with children with special needs. I met my good sister friend Darlene who had a daughter with Down syndrome the same age as Goose. She and I hit it off instantly and we began to talk about ways we could help other mothers in our community. Darlene was so instrumental in my advocacy journey. She showed me how to effectively advocate for Qismah in school and recommended resources that could help enhance her quality of life.

We eventually founded a non-profit organization called Determined To Achieve Parent Network (DTA). This organization was the vehicle to help us create our own lane and address the gaps in addressing the needs of underserved and underrepresented populations in the urban community. We received support from various religious and government agencies to provide arts and crafts and karate to the children with special needs in our community.

Back then New Jersey had many resources for parents to access for their children. And they also created programs for people with disabilities and families to participate in. A few programs that we completed were Project Take Charge (which was discontinued) and Partners in Policy Making (PIP).

PIP is an eight month interactive educational program that trained us in leadership development and advocacy for our children. I learned so much about the Individuals with Disabilities Education Act (also known as IDEA). The Individuals with Disabilities Education Act (IDEA) is a law that makes available a free appropriate public education to eligible children with disabilities throughout the nation and ensures special education and related services to those children.

As you advocate for your child throughout their life, you will be introduced to many acronyms. Prepare yourself by learning as much as you can about the laws that are here to protect people with disabilities. I kept a file of Qismah's immunizations, medical records, and other pertinent information that I could reference when attending IEP (Individualized education plan) meetings at her school.

There are a few lessons I learned along the way as I advocated for my daughter. First, as a mother, I always trusted my intuition. No one knows or knew my daughter better than I did. When I would go to IEP meetings, I always went in being aware of her strengths and what she needed help learning. I also knew that the research that I found specifically for people with Down syndrome would assist me in making the best decisions for her education.

Second, I've also learned throughout the years that Qismah is her own person and that I should not baby her. She wanted her own cell phone and house key. Initially, I was reluctant to get her a house key but she persisted and she was able to establish some independence. That situation taught me to never judge the capabilities of my daughter and to trust that she is able to do more than even I thought possible. She was and still is my greatest teacher.

Biography

Khadija Ali is the mother to 23-year-old Qismah, who was born with Down syndrome. Once Khadija recovered from the shock of her daughter's diagnosis, she committed to learning everything about Down syndrome then made it her life's mission to provide the best quality of life for Qismah. Khadija co-founded the Determined To Achieve (DTA) Parent Network to improve the lives of special needs people and their families through advocacy, education, communication, and raising awareness.

She's also the Founder of Mothers Of Exceptional Children Community Group, an online support group for parents of children with special needs, and the author of the Unwelcome Committee and contributor to Widowed But Not Wounded, an anthology.

As the owner of Be Your Own Kind of Beautiful Coaching, Inc., and the Evelyn Rose Collection, a plus-size boutique, Khadija is passionate about empowering women to discover their own unique kind of beauty.

Khadija and her husband Abdullah co-host the Heal to Love Podcast, where they take listeners on an intimate journey through the highs, lows, and lessons in love and healing. Connect with Khadija at www.exceptionalchildrenbook.com and www.yourkindofbeautiful.com

Acknowledgments

There are so many people along the way that I can name individually and in this space, I will do my best. Charge it to my head and not my heart if I leave out anyone!

I've met so many people in my daughter's twenty-three years who've been instrumental in her growth and foundation. From therapists, teachers, fellow moms of children with different abilities to our family.

To my sons and daughters who've loved their sister like no other, thank you. I know you've all had to sacrifice in a myriad of ways and give your time, love and attention to your sister. Latif, Amir, Medina, and Sulayman, I appreciate you pouring into your sister and being kind and loving.

To the teachers of Bergen County and Englewood Public schools: Ms. Williams, Ms. Salazar, Ms. Arnesen and all of the supporting staff who taught and looked after my daughter over her preschool and elementary school career.

To the teachers and supporting staff of Charles County who taught Qismah over her elementary and middle school,
I appreciate all that you did for her.

And I want to send a special thank you to Qismah's high school teachers and supporting staff at Athens Drive high school: Ms. Serviss, Ms. Nedoma, Mr. Adams, Ms. Fisher, thank you for showing kindness, love, and pouring into Qismah.
She still misses you all so much!

A special shout out to my partner, sister and friend, Darlene Reeves. Darlene, from the moment I met you, I knew we would be lifelong sisters. No matter the time or distance, I love you and Cadena always. Thank you for showing me what partnership and philanthropy truly looks like. Thank you for always leading the way and demonstrating how extraordinary of a life a child with exceptional abilities can have. The way you care for and plan for Cadena's life is a true blueprint.

I would like to thank my first husband, may he continue to rest in peace, A.Karriem Ali for being the best daddy an exceptional little girl could have. When Qismah was born, I asked him what were we going to do? And he simply said, 'Take care of her.' That has stayed with me, especially when he passed away. I knew I had to step up and make sure 'Goose' was good.

The Mothers of Exceptional Children authors: Thank you. You have stayed the course of this book and it took us a long time to get here. Thank you for generously sharing your stories of resilience, vulnerability, strength, and knowledge with the world. It is my belief that the parents, educators, and families who read your journey will gain a deeper understanding of the path you all so valiantly walk every day with your children. Thank you Dr. Abena Asantewaa for enlightening our audience with the psychological expertise and compassion you've displayed in your thirty year career as a school psychologist. And thank you for being a friend, sister, mentor and confidant throughout our friendship.

Yolanda Barnes aka 'Yogii'- I cannot express the amount of appreciation I have for you but let me try. You have brought the vision of Mothers of Exceptional Children to life visually. The amount of changes and revisions we've had; and you always do it with a warm heart and loving energy. If I could clone you, I would! I never shared this with you but your support kept me going during this journey. You demonstrate the ability to do business with a heart and I appreciate you.

To my husband, Abdullah Wilson, you came into my life and embraced all that came with me including Goose. The way you love and care for her is so heartwarming. You exemplify fatherhood with sacrifice, protection, and unconditional love. Thank you babe.

The UP side of Downs

No parent expects to get the diagnosis that the beautiful baby boy they have asked for for their entire life would be born with Down Syndrome. But when I really think about it, I got exactly what I asked for. Absolutely everything I asked for and more. I wanted a little boy that would stay a baby for longer, I could hold him closer for longer and he would never want to leave me. You see, my pregnancy was a breeze, delightful even. For years I'd asked for a boy when I was 35. But after having 3 beautiful daughters very early, and never remarrying, I put that thought right out of my mind. Fast forward, I'm 34 years old and now pregnant with my 4th child. This was in the late 1990', at that time it was standard operating procedure to have the AFP test done (Alpha Fetoprotein) blood test at my age. My results were within normal range +\- 1. Now, if I'd happened to have been 35 years old during my pregnancy and/or had an elevated AFP, it would have been common practice to also get an Amniocentesis (also referred to as an amniotic fluid test). This test was primarily used to detect chromosomal abnormalities and is performed when a woman is between 15 and 20 weeks gestation. This is a more invasive test and could cause unwanted issues, mainly, preterm labor or spontaneous abortion. Because I was only 34 during the pregnancy and my AFP was within range, it was not suggested for me to have the Amnio, in any event, I would have never risked my baby' health to find out something that I already know would not make any difference in my decision to keep what was being given to me. After all, I really did ask for him, exactly the way he was.

I worked literally until the day I went into labor. After a few very strong contractions, out comes my little boy, so quiet, but eyes wide open. I don't even remember him crying, he was just happy to be here! This all happened so fast, my primary doctor didn't have time to get there. I do remember the look on the on-call doctor' face was strange, but nothing registered in my mind. My oldest daughter Keeyawna was with me, we both thought he looked just like her. And of course he still does look exactly like all of us.

It all started with his APGAR number being too low, this is the score doctors use to quickly evaluate the health of all newborns at 1 and 5 minutes after birth. Kameron wasn't able to regulate his body temperature, and they detected a slight heart murmur. Thinking back on it, he looks just like a typical Down Syndrome baby, chunky and cute, flat nose and protruding tongue and all, but I didn't see it yet, but they were very aware of these normal Down Syndrome characteristics. Nobody officially said anything, but me having worked in hospital settings for many many years prior to his birth, I now realize that as medical professionals, you can't always say what you think you know, you need to have the appropriate test, documentation and scientific proof, also known as Karyotype Test (see illustration). I had many times been on the other side of that conversation, and already knew all too well what the test would reveal or what the diagnosis would be, but understood that there was a level of genetic testing that would need to occur and have a written proof and verification. Still everyone was just very concerned with his core temperature. Also, all the nurses keep coming in checking him, nurses that weren't assigned to my room. I thought it was because they all knew a real Angel had just arrived! You know, like how the 3 wisemen and all the animals dropped by to see their new baby King, in the Jesus story. It will take several weeks, and several well baby check up appointments before I would get the official diagnosis of trisomy 21. This is a very specific type of Down Syndrome, 1 of 3 types. I wasn't disappointed at that point, I had done a little research honestly, and felt like if I had my choice of the 3 types, it would have been Mosaic, not Trisomy, I'm not really sure why I felt that way. It sounds silly now, but you know how it is when you think you have a choice of something, I wanted the Cadillac of Down Syndrome if I was going to have to deal with any of them at all. Even now I laugh at that assumption.

Kameron' Karyotype Test Results

KARYOTYPE: 47, XY, +21

Finally my doctor arrived. I remember he looked very worried, he asked to see Kameron, and if I had a name for him. He then asked if I had any regrets about not getting the Amnio test? He was concerned that if I would have known during the pregnancy that Kameon would be born with Down Syndrome that I may have chosen to terminate my pregnancy or made arrangements to give him up for adoption.

I could not for the life of me understand what he was talking about. I was offended that he thought I would have ever considered something that ridiculous. He went on and on about how much medical attention, the many potential medical issues, psychological, physical, and emotional impairments that he could potentially have and that it would be very difficult for me. He said it would be totally understandable if I would want to give him up for adoption and the hospital could set all of that up before I went home. I remember him saying I didn't even have to take him home with me -- as if! I don't even remember what my response was, but knowing me, back then, his face was probably very red when he left my room, I don't think I saw him again until my 2 month check up.

After the 2nd priest and 3rd social worker stopped by my room to check in on me, absolving me of all guilt and shame, I told the nurse that the next person that walked into my room with that bullshit was gonna crawl out tail first. And if you know me, then you already know.

In the beginning, I did not seek any outside resources whatsoever. I was a 3 time award winning mother of 3 amazing daughters, ages 17, 16, and 15. I had worked in the medical field extensively and had seen plenty of babies and small children in my community who were born with Down Syndrome. I thought, how much different could it be? He's a baby, he needs what every baby needs, right?

I was given tons of resources and literature on Down Syndrome before I left the hospital. However, the only book I was given to take home was a 1962 version of a book written by Dr. John Langdon Down. Although he wasn't the one who first discovered this chromosomal abnormality, he was the first to describe it and the cluster symptoms that are associated with Down's Syndrome. By today's standards, this book would not make the reading list, it used terms such as "idiot" "Mongoloid idiot" and "mental retardation",

it had a very low to no expectation of what my son's life could be. Even back then, I knew that most references and definitely the language being used to describe these beautiful souls, left a lot to be desired, I personally was offended that they would've even put something like that in writing and publish it, let alone give to new parents.

Needless to say, I left that book exactly where they laid it in my hospital room, it's probably still there. If you think about the level of sensitivity from the 90s to today, a lot has changed for the better. About 3 or 4 years after Kameron was born I actually ran across an updated version of this book, sadly not much has changed however the language describing them had been changed from "idiot" and "Mongoloid idiot" to Down Syndrome. Good for them!

Once I got to Georgia, because of all of the difficulties with the new ADA regulations in California, I had become quite an advocate for my son, a lot of the times questioning why they hadn't already done something very early on knowing that in that moment it had nothing to do with Kameron but it soon would, and I wanted to get it resolved before we got to that juncture.

It was through advocating for him I begin to understand that a lot of the fight, a lot of the push, and a lot of the work needed to be done to pave the way for him for the rest of his life. And with most things that I am interested in I became very good at advocating first for my child then for everyone in my child's classrooms, and then for everyone associated with anything I wanted my son to be associated with.

We have been blessed to have been sent a tribe of parents, professionals and doctors along the way as Kameron has grown up. This tribe was able to share with me their knowledge and information of what worked for them or what I would need to do to prepare for something in the future. I am a firm believer that any information that would benefit my son must be shared with others, the more of us that know how to advocate and seek services and interventions for our children the better life that they can have.

I have always prided myself as being a source of good information. Rarely will I say "I don't know", although I may not know, I am about to find out and if I know then so will the next parent. Information, resources and the ability to utilize them has been one of the most valuable Super Powers I have been granted being a parent of an Exceptional One. I never stop asking "how" "why" and "why not".

It is all about perspective and deciding if you are gonna create the life you want based on the cards you are dealt or if you are gonna accept whatever society says with no questions. I chose to be the Creatress of my life. Of course parenting an exceptional child impacts your life, but I really don't think Kameron' special needs had much of a negative impact on my life back then, especially when he was younger. The bottom line was I was a single parent with a new baby, and even though over the first 8 years there were a lot of hospital stays a lot of doctors trips, being single allowed me and my daughters to deal with it as a collective unit.

I didn't have the usual issues with a partner who didn't share any biological DNA with my son, and may not want to support us through it.

I was single before I had him and I was single after I had him so the way I approached it was exactly that. Now, as he got older I was a little more aware of attachment issues he developed very early and realized that for the same and different reasons not everyone I met would be worthy of meeting my son. So from that perspective I guarded and protected his energetics space fiercely, they may know I have a son, they may know he has Down Syndrome, they may even know what he looks like from photos, (he was always a cutie patutie and I was very proud he chose me to be his maternal guide on his journey, so I always had lots of pictures of him) however, they would never meet him unless I thought highly enough of them to gift them with an introduction. I have since realized that no matter the time frame, no matter the circumstances, once you meet my son he will make an impact on your life today or in the future, you will never be the same. And not everyone deserves to have that revelation, but if you have had the privilege of meeting him, count yourself exceptional.

Prior and during my pregnancy I worked as an executive secretary for the utility company in that state, a very affluent position, and I loved it, I could not see myself doing anything else. However, once he was born and having quite a few serious medical crises right away, I decided to take a sabbatical, a one-year leave of absence. I had saved up quite a bit of money earlier on being single. I didn't know what to expect but wanted to be financially prepared. I had more than enough savings to take off for at least a year. At some point during my sabbatical I realized I never wanted to have to leave him, and started trying to figure out ways to stay at home. Back in the late 90s being an entrepreneur wasn't a real big thing. I didn't have a lot of friends or family members who were doing that, everybody was worker bees and worked outside of the home.

A friend of mine mentioned to me that I was good with kids and that I should start a daycare for children with special needs since I was having such a difficult time finding reliable childcare myself. Actually, the friend was the only home child care that Kameron attended. Her name was Miss Jackie, she said, it was harder on me leaving him everyday than it was on him being left. I felt so guilty putting him off on someone else. He had a list of 14 medications and to medical machince that he might need during the day. One thing turned into another and in late 2000 she helped me opened up my own daycare. That was the beginning of my entrepreneurship, I haven't worked for very many companies for very long since then and to this day what I choose to do for business and pleasure completely revolves around Kameron and his needs, making sure that I never have to check in with anyone, or get permission to take him anywhere, I don't have to check in with anyone who really don't care about me, to inform them that my son is in the hospital and I don't know how long it's going to be before he's released. Realizing that I could support myself while being able to take great care of him every single day has been one of the best revelations I could have ever made.

Kameron and my desire to really be present in his everyday life helped me understand early in my life that the purpose for each of us being here would not be what society wants us to think it is. Life is not about working every day at 9 to 5 or putting in extra time at someone else's company making someone else get rich just so that you can maybe pay your bills. Life was never supposed to be getting up every single day dreading going to the place that you must go to in order to feed and provide for your family. There's actually something that we are very good at that we came here to do, something that makes us happy and may even afford us the opportunity to create a different life. We called that a "hobby or a side gig", something that we don't get paid very much if anything at all. Because of the path my life took after Kameron was born, it allowed me to seek the opportunities to be creative and think out of the box, not within the confines that society wanted to keep me in.

I operated my home daycare for almost 10 years, from California to Georgia. That afforded me the chance to be at every field trip, every doctor's appointment, every hospital stay, every extracurricular activity for him and not have to worry about losing my job or not having enough money to make ends meet. It taught me how to be self-sufficient and what was really important and that was showing up every single day with a smile on my face to do something that I love, and that was to watch, to witness, to protect and fiercely advocate for him every single day. It wouldn't always be easy, but it would pay off in ways I could have never imagined.

Here is the Up Side Of Downs: You see, the fact is Kameron was born with Down Syndrome, he will live his entire life with Down Syndrome, and when he leaves this place, he will leave it with the trait of Down Syndrome, but that does not define or limit who he is. Very early on I knew that he had a right to have the life that anyone else would choose to have, even though he may not understand how to make those choices. In high school, I wanted him to participate in every extracurricular activity and to have access to friends and social events. I wanted him to have his senior year in high school and be able to do the most!

I wanted him to be included with every senior activity, have beautiful senior pictures, attend Jr. and Senior prom with a date, and wear his class ring. I wanted him to have his senior locker decorated so that people could see he wasn't any different than they were. I wanted my son to walk across the stage and receive his diploma like every other high school graduate, and YES he did all that! Believe it or not when we first moved to Georgia that was not an option for him to graduate with his class and walk across the stage to officially receive his diploma. The way it was originally set up is after his senior year he would go onto a secondary education more of a life skills situation, to teach him how to transition into adulthood, but he would never walk across the stage with his graduating class.

He would just get a piece of paper later on after the fact. Now, anybody that knows me knows we weren't going to have that. It was an uphill battle but by the time he got to high school, all of that had changed and he was able to have all of these wonderful experiences, The same experiences you, I and every other high school student had in high school.

Kameron is now a happy, healthy 25 year old young man. I often look at his life and think, if I get a chance to do this all over again I want to come back as Kameron. I know it might sound strange to some. Let's be honest, Kam had a rough start, a bumpy beginning, there were a lot of unknowns and challenges that he would face in his young life. He has met every challenge and overcome the odds of some of the most knowledgeable professionals this world has to offer. I promise you if you look in any book, you will never find another person who has such a beautiful and amazing life as he does. Kameron wakes up every morning with a smile on his face, laughing and giggling and talking trash (his absolute most favorite thing in the world to do). His day is filled with joy, love, leisure and lots of laughing. He goes to bed every night laughing, giggling and talking trash. Kameron loves talking trash, and he's good at it too.

Kameron has been a Special Olympics athlete since he was 8 years old. During his school years he participated in Special Olympics, every 3 months there's a different sport and at the end of the 3 months the reward was you got to go to a State Games. If you've never been to a special Olympic state game before, it is a beautiful site. Imagine young children and adults of every age from all over the state, with every different living ability, coming together to participate in the sport of their choice. They compete against other special Olympic athletes for a gold, silver or bronze medal. Every participant gives 110% of themselves. They have a simple motto:

**"Let me win.
But if I cannot win, let me be brave in the attempt."**

Imagine having this experience year after year for 16+ years! Do you understand the community that they create by participating and attending, by being both a spectator and athlete, and cheering on their friends. The beautiful extended family that they have at their finger tips. The life long friends that he has made on his journey are like family. This will be his life for as long as he is able to participate, his impact on the world, his gift to the world is to share love, smiles and hugs, to inspire and provoke positive thoughts in all who are blessed to cross his path.

Looking back to where this beautiful journey began, I wish someone would have told me, it was ok to let go of unrealistic expectations that society tries to impose on every parent. That it is okay that he won't meet someone else's "ages and stages", goals and developmental milestones. They should have told me that he will set his own standards, make his own goals, and reach his own milestones that would be in perfect timing and in tune for who he was as an individual.

I could have used the knowledge that developing tough skin was a badge of honor not a curse. See, when the system fails to support you as a caretaker of a child with different abilities, when society failed to conceive the answers ahead of time so that when you presented with the many questions of "how" "why" and "where", they had no response, thick skin would be necessary to not get distracted anger and feel defeated.

We relocated from CA to GA when Kameron was 5yrs old. Here in GA, there is something called the Medicaid waiver. I didn't really understand it but I did sign him when I arrived, but no one told me how tremendously beneficial that would prove to be as he approached adulthood.

I wish I would have known about the Special Olympic community, and all of the great works that they do for our young adults, from the start of school throughout their entire life. I wish I would've known all those years when I was donating to United Way, that what I should have been donating to was the local Downs Syndrome Association in my area to support the livelihood, the leisure and social skills that my son would be a part of one day, and to advocate with my friends and family heavily for them to do the same.

I wish they would have told me that he would be the best thing in my life I never knew I needed. They should have told me, "this one will challenge everything you thought you knew, and grow you on the journey you were born for". They should have told me, I was highly thought of, that in spite of all other obstacles I was going to face in life, I unknowingly would be able to rise to the occasion of being the parent of this Exceptional One. And the reward for that is the smile on his face, the twinkle in his eyes, and the joy in his laugh every single day of my life.

Biography

Meet Sharalene Wheeler-Reaves Certified Hydro Steam, Womb Reiki Practitioner, New Usui Reiki Master Teacher, Founder School of Holistic Health & Wellness, Womb Warrior Training. I am a mother of 4 beautiful souls, 3 daughters; 41, 40, and 39, and my amazing son Kameron, 24yo. I am originally from Fresno, CA but relocated to the Atlanta area in 2013. I have been blessed to manifest the relationship of my dreams with an amazing man. We have been together for 5 years in this dimension, but it feels as if our souls have happily danced together for many lifetimes before.

My greatest passion and desire is to assist myself in healing by guiding other women (my tribe) to their own healing, to create a safe magical community of support through womb/selfcare.

Women experience a plethora of unavoidable and many times unspoken traumas in their lifetime; many of which lead to both their lives and health unraveling.

I work with and serve women of all ages and stages of life:
>Adult women (the mothers)
>Young women (the moon babies)
>Wise women (the elders)

to foster a healthy perspective of themselves and begin to strengthen the relationships in their lives with the sisters and women in their tribe, as well as with the husbands and children in their community. The ultimate goal is to see ourselves as healthy, whole, complete and worthy of love so that the healing can take place.

I believe that we are all individuals and take different approaches to our healing. The path to restoration is as individual as the person walking their path. Knowing this I diligently trained in several natural womb healing modalities including Tantra, Womb and New Usui Reiki, and Crystal Supported Herbal Yoni Steaming. I practice this cross-modality therapy based on medicinal herbs, spices and gemstone therapy to heal and repair the sacred womb that is inside of every woman.

Finally, my life mission is twofold:
to educate and facilitate the integration of mind, body and spirit connection to awaken the feminine consciousness by healing the world from the outside in, one womb at a time.

For More Information or To Book Sharalene For Your Next Event:
Email: **Sharalene@nfysoaps.com**
FB: Sharalene Wheeler, **@NaturallyNFY**, **@nfysohhw** or visit my website **www.nfysoaps.com**
Phone: 470-687-5744

Acknowledgments

They say it takes a community to raise a child. Well before I found that community, there were others who stood in the gap to help me along and find my way. I would like to thank a few of who supported, walked with, and still walk with us everyday on our journey. I am so very grateful for all the love and support from each and everyone of them.

To the amazing young women I am blessed to walk this life path with as my "3 Heart Beats". Keeyawna, Kiesha and Kalea, who have always stood by me, with me and for me. I could not begin to imagine my life as a single parent of an Exceptional One without each of them.
They embraced the decisions I made with openness and compassion, and surrounded Kameron always with so much love and support. Not only was he blessed with 3 wonderful sisters but 3 additional mommies that would teach, love and protect him in their own unique ways. I am eternally grateful for their love and constant support from the very beginning. Kameron broke their hearts wide open and they each allowed him to teach them to be non judgmental, and compassionate of all exceptional ones. Thank you for holding me up when I was down, riding with me when I had lost my way, and always believing we are stronger and better for our journey together. 1-4-3 to the moon and beyond the stars, from this life to the next

In 2003 I met a beautiful soul by the name of Dawn Hobbins, she was Kameron' K-5 grade teacher. I lovingly called her his "daytime Mom".
She rode in the ambulance with Kameron on more than one occasion, and stayed by his side until I could get there. She has baby sat him for years without allowing me to pay her. She introduced him to the world of Special Olympics and stood with him for years until he understood that this would become the community where he would flourish and shine. She has taught me so much about standing up and advocating for his rights, and how to help those around us see him for more than his different abilities but for the wonderful amazing and unique person he was becoming.

She is so much more than just a friend, "she will always be family." Thank you for loving and advocating for my son as if he were your own from the moment you met him. For all of the guidance, support and assistance you gave me navigating the Gwinnett County, GA educational system. Thank you for being the extended family to me and all of my children when we moved over 2500 miles to call Georgia our home. You demonstrated how to advocate and work within the system to get everything that Kameron deserved to become a happy, productive and loving human being. Your heart is so big and beautiful and I love you from the bottom of mine. Thank you!

To my partner in life, Kenneth Reaves, Ph.D. this is the man that would show up in my life and fiercely love, protect, teach and spoil Kameron. He has been thoughtful, supportive and a great spiritual guide in our lives. He is the dream I've dreamt for years and years, the lover, life partner and friend I manifested to share our lives with. Everyday has been a wonderful adventure for us to share. He wakes up and figues out how to make us smile, and to provide an incredibly extra-ordinary life for us, I thank you for seeing our son for the amazing and exceptional person he is, for making and creating space in your heart just for him. For your extraordinary ability to be open to the never ending process of creating our beautiful family that is "#TeamLivinDaLife",

I love you and will carry you with me always.

Lastly, to my son Kameron. Thank you for choosing to have me be your guide in this life. Because of you, I am who I was fully created to be. You gave me purpose to live out loud and on purpose, with no apology. You have shown me how to be a more active, loving and patient parent. Thank you for not allowing me to push my overrated expectations on you, but support you in wherever your heart leads you. I can't imagine my life without you just the way you are. You are the picture of **The Up Side of Downs**, you are my moon, my sun and my entire galaxy. The sun truly rises and sets with your smile. I am the luckiest Mommy in the world to have been chosen to walk this journey forever holding your hand. To my Nunnie Butt-Butt, 1-4-3 in this life and every life after, til infinity and beyond.

Early Intervention

If you, your child's doctor, or other care provider is concerned about your child's development, ask to be connected with your state or territory's early intervention program to find out if your child can get services to help. If your doctor is not able to connect you, you can reach out yourself. A doctor's referral is not necessary.

If your child is under age 3: Call your state or territory's early intervention program and say: "I have concerns about my child's development and I would like to have my child evaluated to find out if he/she is eligible for early intervention services."

Early intervention is available in all 50 states including: American Samoa, Commonwealth of the North Marianna Islands, Puerto Rico and US Virgin Islands.
For more information:
https://www.cdc.gov/ncbddd/actearly/parents/states.html

United Cerebral Palsy

United Cerebral Palsy (UCP) is a non-profit organization that provides a variety of services to children and adults with cerebral palsy. It is an advocacy organization for those who have cerebral palsy and their families.
For more information: **https://ucp.org/**

Autism Navigator

Autism Navigator was created by faculty and staff in the Autism Institute at the Florida State University College of Medicine. Learn more about the research projects in the FSU Autism Institute that contributed to the content of Autism Navigator-the FIRST WORDS® Project and the Early Social Interaction Project (ESI).
https://autismnavigator.com/family-resources/

Gigi's Playhouse
Gigi's Playhouse is a 501c3 non-profit organization that provides FREE programs for people with down syndrome. GiGi's Playhouse was created to change the way the world views a Down syndrome diagnosis and send a global message of acceptance for all.
https://gigisplayhouse.org/

National Down Syndrome Society
800-221-4602
http://www.ndss.org/

Special Olympics
http://www.specialolympics.org

Easter Seals
http://www.easterseals.com

Autism In Black
http://www.autisminblack.org

National Association for Down Syndrome
http://www.nads.org/

National Info Center for Children & Youth w/ Disabilities:
1-800-695-0285
http://www.nichcy.org/

Partners in Policymaking
Partners in Policymaking is a free program, available in forty-nine states, designed to teach people with disabilities and family members the power of advocacy to positively change the way people with disabilities are supported, viewed, taught, live and work. Check with your state's website or google 'Partners in Policymaking + your state' to learn more about the program.

To The Readers:

We thank you for purchasing this book. It was a true labor of love. We want the parents of children with exceptional abilities to know that they are not alone. There are resources and other families who know this walk intimately. We, the authors, have cried, experienced fear of the unknown and felt despair. We have been exhausted at the level of care that is required for our children. We want you to know that it can get better. Please hold on and know that your child can have the best life possible for them. Hold and create a vision and use the resources and support available to you. We are including a few resources that helped us along the way. And if ever need support, reach out to any of us.

We will help.

www.ingramcontent.com/pod-product-compliance
Lightning Source LLC
Chambersburg PA
CBHW050915160426
43194CB00011B/2421